Grasping At Honesty

A Poetry Collection

B. Nantz

Made with ❤ on the BookLeaf Publishing Platform

www.bookleafpub.in

www.bookleafpub.com

Dedication

For my sisters,
Kaelyn and *Bethany*.
You are my universe. You always have been.

Preface

Dear Reader,

I desperately hope you may find a place to call home
within these words.
Dog-ear the pages; light a candle; write your own;
sticky-note them on your mirror;
find a prayer within them; eat them for breakfast.
I know I have and I do.
I end these pages with an 'amen.' I hope you do, too.

B.

Acknowledgements

To everyone who has shown me love and care, and
encouraged me in my work,
thank you for giving me the courage to share my words
with the world.
Thank you for sharing your listening ears and gentle
hands.
They guide me through this messy life.

B.

1. Unpeeling

I unpeel myself
Amid citrus
Before you
Bravely
From beneath
The layers that held me

2. Bright in the Room

Bright in the room
I slept in
Drowsy thoughts
Still stringing themselves together

The morning's coffee
Dark, deep, rich
Slowly sipped

Bright in the room
Rattan, live plants
Butterflies, off-whites
I, still finding my color

6. Pressed Violets

This life
Presses me,
As a lifeless violet
Between pristine pages:
Gold-edge lyricism

4. Androgony

[Her] form
Illuminated by moonlight
Grieving
For all she wished to be
Was androgyny

5. "Atypical"

The lining of my throat
Screaming
With what you call
'Disability'
Stuck inside
Unsure why
I must fight for
'Typicality'
When you could
Accept me

6. Pain, in Chronicity

There's a sigh
In the deepest part of me
Grateful for what used to be
What *I* used to be
I didn't used to feel
So ashamed
Of me
It didn't used to be
So hard
To walk
On a Monday's
Afternoon breath

7. Mercies of the Morn'

When I see the world
Outside this sun-dusted
Window
May it not be thorough
The lens of
Tuesday's tension headache
But through grace:
Never-ceasing, Ever-prevaling,
Ever-providing
May each panel of glass
Become a schema of faith
I gaze through,
But not past-
The open space
Of love-steeped
Sacrifice
May this be
My dwelling place
I declare:
No analog wasted,

No emotion unheard,
I, faith-filled,
Frosted with
The mercy of a new morn'

8. Panic for Breakfast

These wounds
Skin made raw
By *panic* and
Uncertainty is
The salt
Waltzing
In it...
How...
Therapeutic

9. In Transit

The snow is gentle
On Tuesday
With coffee and hiccups
Waiting on friends
To answer texts
Waiting on life
To answer uncertainty
They don't;
It doesn't
And so I wait
With the fluff-like
Snow
For sun
To melt me

10. Oak, Mahogany, Ash

My insides are
A mahogany swirl
Of anxious and
Solution-drawn
An old drawer's been
Opened,
Its handle dusted
With the essence of
Yesterdays
Archived

Soft, vulnerable palms
Ache
Not to touch,
Having only recently healed
From its contents
The tissue still new,
In vulnerability, sensitive:

I don't want to touch it
I don't want it opened
I don't want to cough

At its dustiness
Releasing into my
Atmosphere
My own
Oaky eyes
Will darken
Just looking at it

The slip from
Oak to
Mahogany to
Ash is
So delicate
I've seen it
A million times
Before

11. On Hope

May creation come close
To your
Fingers and toes
Whether through
Reckless giggles or
Pain-speckled prose
May hope rest as a
Gentle hand
On your back: warm

You may be drained: dry
Now
Not forever,
As everything 'round floods in
And bleeds out
May heaven
Come close
To your soul
Instilling into all your lack:
Hope

12. In Sickness, In Health

Sandwiched between
The world of the sick
And the world of the healthy
I seek peace
In solitude:
A park-city cafe solo
And a half-enjoyed
Cappucino
Between the used bookstore,
The dentist, and
The cafe on the corner,
So my thoughts are
Stacked
Like books vertical
Before heading to the hospital
I can't help but wonder
Where I'll be
A few months from now

13. Caffeinated, Baptismal

Tucked into
Gingham and silk
I've now arisen
From Monday
Into Tuesday
Baptized by
Coffee, NPR
An article from a friend
Thoughts between
Sweet, warm sips
Spirit, God, Universe:
Meet me in the stillness
Distracted, I crave to connect

14. Tide's Settle

A victory: survival
Most days I forget
To realize
These days

The old, bitter
Taste in my mouth
Since dissipated
Almost neutral,
Something I don't mind
Too much

The days
The world was
Too heavy
For my neck
I could barely
Hold it up

Now, I hold my head

High, most times
I've even a new haircut
I wear its lightness, wavyness
With pride

Though, I'm still
Fuzzy, nauseous
I'm peaceful:
A triumph through
Solitude
I hope beyond
Each platitude

Somewhere
Along the way
Normalcy settled
Peace in the brokenness;
Of ordinary
Between blood draws and
Heart monitors
I find sanctuary

I am grateful
For all I'm afforded
Some level of health,
To experience
Life in color

I've never lost my spark
No matter how life
Runs me over

15. Origami

Life feels
As delicate as
The origami butterflies
Strung before my
East-facing
Window

16. "Fighter"

My body is
A soldier
I hate
Everything
About that

17. Mostly-Cooled Coffee

I

Am the

Mostly-cooled coffee

At the bedside or

Left on the kitchen table

With the newspaper crossword,

Unattempted

I hold the residual temperature

Of lingering warmth,

Praying my

Little is

Enough;

Praying my

Tiny hope

Will settle at the top of my cup

Where steam once danced

I

Am the

Mostly-cooled coffee

With only a few

Sips left

18. Citrus Season

Citrus season:
Blooming
One of them
Persimmon
Sweet with honey,
Sweet like you
Let God
Peel back the
Layers
Until all that's left is
Him, you

19. Poetry for Breakfast

Some days I
Read poetry
Others, I
Eat it,
Hungry for
Honesty
Something real as
Birdsong come
Seven in the morn'

20. On Trauma

I cannot undo
My survivalist's heart;
What made my needs
Into a rug
For what
Created them so
Cannot be undone

21. Grief to Bloom

As sun shining through lace curtains,
So my shortcomings allow space
For the spring to find its way
Through me
May its warmth heal each winter's ache:
Every grief

The winter weathered me
As water running deeply
Along the streamside
Its current strong within
Softened my edges have become
Internal and external
I am not as sharp as I once was
Adamant on image,
Overwhelmed by the same

Awakening has begun
As bulbs deep in the earth
Hope is swelling within me

In the gentlest of forms
May it also
Find its way to bloom;
May I

www.ingramcontent.com/pod-product-compliance
Lightning Source LLC
Chambersburg PA
CBHW071239140726
47996CB00007B/2680